Summ of

Circe
Madeline Miller

Conversation Starters

By BookHabits

Bonus Downloads
*Get Free Books with **<u>Any Purchase</u>** of* Conversation Starters!

Every purchase comes with a FREE download!

Add spice to any conversation
Never run out of things to say
Spend time with those you love

Scan Your Phone

Tips for Using Conversation Starters:

EVERY GOOD BOOK CONTAINS A WORLD FAR DEEPER THAN the surface of its pages. Questions herein are designed to bring us beneath the surface of the page and invite us into the world that lives on. These questions can be used to:

- Foster a deeper understanding of the book
- Promote an atmosphere of discussion for groups
- Assist in the study of the book, either individually or corporately
- Explore unseen realms of the book as never seen before

Table of Contents

Introducing *Circe* 6

Discussion Questions 13

Introducing the Author 34

Fireside Questions 40

Quiz Questions 51

Quiz Answers 64

Ways to Continue Your Reading 65

Introducing *Circce*

CIRCE IS THE NEWEST FICTION NOVEL FROM the internationally bestselling author of *The Song of Achilles*, Madeline Miller. *The Song of Achilles* retold the epic Troy through the eyes of Patroclus, whose death launched the duel between Achilles and Hector. His death was avenged and Achilles dragged Hector's body in victory. Miller's *Circe,* on the other hand, was inspired from Homer's *The Odyssey*.

Circe, was born as the firstborn of the mightiest of titans, Helios and the beautiful nymph Perse. Though her father is the god of the sun, she did not look nor speak like a god. Her own father describes her as dull. She is often dismissed as unattractive. The sound of her thin voice offended the gods. Because her features do not match her divinity, she was rejected by her more beautiful, more majestic kin. She was treated harshly because she was different. Her inferior status among the gods led her to isolation. Her isolation led her to mortals. She found acceptance in a land that is not her own. As she walked with mortals, she discovered witchcraft, a power forbidden to the gods.

Circe then witnessed how the gods harshly treated Prometheus. His plight moved her and caused her to sympathize more with the humans. Not long after, Circe meets another human who will make her fall in love. He was a fisherman named Glaucos. His love makes her use witchcraft despite it being forbidden to gods. She made a pharmaka, magical herbs that activate sorcery, to keep Glaucos from his mortality. Glaucos becomes a towering, green-haired, trident-wielding god. With new power in his fingertips, her grows tired of plain Circe and transfers his attentions to the beautiful viper-hearted sea-nymph Scylla. Circe was heartbroken and her love turn to rage. She used witchcraft upon Scylla and turned her into a hideous monster of the sea. She then exiled her rival in love to an unpopulated island.

When Zeus found out that Circe used witchcraft to cast a dark spell, he banished Circe to the remote island of Aiaia. She used her isolation to harness her dark power. She drew strength from nature and her power grew stronger and stronger. Aiaia may be a place of exile but it is destined to be the passageway of many whose fates will intertwine with hers. Hermes, the messenger god; Daedalus, the craftsman and the legendary ship bearing the golden fleece, passed through Aiaia. It is also here where Odysseus finds her while on his voyage home. Odysseus found her surrounded by tame wolves, swine and lions. She bewitched them after breaking free from a sea captain who attempted to rape her. Circe was famous for turning men into half swine after giving them cheese and wine. Odysseus' crew were no different. Their hunger left them susceptible to Crice's powers. Thus she turned them all into swine but through Eurylochus' warning, Odysseus comes to rescue his men. He was then intercepted by Hermes, the messenger God. He warned Odysseus of Circe's powers and told him to use the herb moly to protect himself. When he resisted Circe and her wizardry, he drew his sword and motioned to attack her. Circe was drawn to him instantly and asked him to bed. Affection quickly grows between these two. Circe afterwards became Odysseus' adviser. Her directions would lead his crew to Scylla and routes that ring familiar through Greek mythology. Circe's love affair with Odysseus would make her different.

Soon after, she finds herself "the proud witch undone before the hero's sword."

Miller's reimagining of Circe is centered around the emotional life of a woman. From her childhood in the house of Helios to her womanhood in the island of Aiaia, Miller paints a goddess whose longing for love and acceptance cause her to lust for men and gods alike. Circe was once a mute character in the Greek mythology. Mythology has vilified Circe for centuries as the cunning witch of Aiaia but Madeline Miller successfully reimagine the life and love of a goddess.

In *Circe*, Miller delved into the great stories of antiquity and wrote a collage of *Odyssey, Argonautica* and *Telegony*. Miller paints a different perspective of the tales we have known for ages. *Circe* is a representation of the classics from the perspective of a woman in the form of a goddess. *The Observer* describes *Circe* "a feminist slant on the Odyssey." *Stylist* praises Miller's depiction of the goddess's immensely relatable humanity, her female strength is displayed "in all its fractured, fragiled glory." *Attitude* called Madeline Miller "an alchemist with words and hailed *Circe* as one of the best and most rewarding books of 2018.

Discussion Questions

"Get Ready to Enter a New World"

Tip: Begin with questions dealing with broader issues to ensure ample time for quality discussions. Read through all discussion questions before engaging.

question 1

Circe was born to Helios, the god of the sun and Perse, a beautiful nymph. Her appearance and her voice were an offensive surprise to her kin. Describe Circe's appearance and voice. Why were her appearance and voice offensive to the gods?

~~~

question 2

Circe was born into a majestic kin but she never felt that she belonged. Why did Circe feel that she did not belong? How did her kin treat her?

~~~

~~~

question 3

Circe is divine in blood but her heart is human. What caused this goddess to turn into humans for acceptance? What did Circe witness that made her sympathize with humans?

~~~

~~~

question 4

Glaucos was a simple fisherman who made Circe fall in love. How did Glaucos and Circe meet? What sparked their attraction to each other?

~~~

question 5

As Circe walked with humans, she discovered witchcraft and learned to wield spells on her own. How did she discover witchcraft? Why did she desire a power that is forbidden to gods?

question 6

Love make people do foolish things. Though a goddess, Circe was no different. She was lovestruck and she wielded a spell for Glaucos. What spell did she cast on Glaucos? What was her motivation for doing so?

~ ~ ~

question 7

Upon receiving the spell, Glaucos turned her eyes to the beautiful Scylla. How did Scylla and Glaucos meet? What made Glaucos forget his love for Circe and leave her for Scylla?

~ ~ ~

~~~

question 8

Enraged by jealousy, Circe turns Scylla into a six-headed hideous monster. How did Glaucos respond to Circe's fit of jealousy? Why did Circe opt to spare Scylla's life and turn her into a monster instead?

~~~

question 9

Zeus found out about Circe's involvement with witchcraft and the spells she wielded on Glaucos and Scylla. Zeus banished Circe into Aiaia. How did Zeus find out about Circe's witchcraft? Why did Zeus banish her into this island, with the knowledge that this is a passageway to many islands?

~ ~ ~

~~~

question 10

Circe learned to harness her power while in Aiaia. How did she harness the power of nature? What other things did Circe do while in exile in Aiaia?

~~~

question 11

Aiaia is a passageway of many ships. Circe was always visited by ships that pass through the island. Who were the notable Greek mythology figures who chanced to pass through her island?

~ ~ ~

~~~

question 12

Odysseus met Circe in Aiaia. She was surrounded by tame swine, lions and wolves. In Greek mythology, what does she do to men who visit her island? Why does she do so?

~~~

question 13

Miller's Circe has an unsatiable lust for men. She takes every chance she can with the gods who visit her island. Who were the gods whom Circe invited to bed? Did she have an offspring because of her relations?

~~~

question 14

Circe develops an attraction with Odysseus. She acted as his guide to his voyage. Describe the routes Circe advises to Odysseus' journey home. Which of the routes did Odysseus take? Why did he choose this among the others?

~~~

question 15

Circe's death came from a hero's sword. Who killed the goddess Circe? What made her vulnerable to this attack? What was the motivation behind the murder?

question 16

Psychologies describes *Circe* "a mesmerizing, fiercely feminist" retelling of a famous Greek mythology story. Is *Circe* a feminist novel? How is a novel characterized as feminist?

~~~

question 17

Toast Book Club recognizes *Circe's* quest for love and acceptance. They say that this "will ring a chord with men and women alike." Why is Circe's character very relatable to today's readers?

~~~

~~~

question 18

Sunday Times Magazine praises Miller's quality of writing and the timeliness of the novel. Why is this novel timely to this generation of readers?

~~~

question 19

Circe is "a life-affirming tale of astonishing beauty" according to *Toast Book Club*. How is Circe life-affirming? What are the points in the novel that is life-affirming to the readers?

question 20

Guardian praises Miller's narrative in *Circe* and describes it as "a supple, pitched in a register that bridges man and myth." How was Miller successful in bridging man and myth in her novel *Circe*?

Introducing the Author

MADELINE MILLER IS AN AMERICAN NOVELIST. Fifteen years prior to her successful writing career, she taught Latin, Greek and Shakespeare to high school students. She earned her bachelor's and master's degrees in Classics from Brown University. She also studied in the Dramaturgy department at Yale School of Drama. Her study focus was the adaptation of classical texts to modern context. She has also attended University of Chicago's Committee on Social Thought.

In 2012, Miller released her first novel, *The Song of Achilles*. Miller reimagines Greece in the age of Heroes. She retells The Illiad through the eyes of Patroclus. Patroclus is an ungainly young prince who lives in the shadow of King Peleus and the great Achilles.

Achilles is glorious and he is the golden son of King Peleus. He is strong, majestic and deemed as the best of all the Greeks. He is a child of a goddess. Patroclus is nothing like Achilles. But one fateful day, Achilles takes Patroclus under his wing. Patroclus develops trust and a steadfast friendship with Achilles. The two develop their skills and passion for the art of war and medicine. As they grow together, Achilles and Patroclus develops a far deeper bond that elicits the displeasure of Achilles

mother Thetis. The cruel goddess of the sea has a

long-standing hatred of mortals.

Their bond will soon be tested as the word

comes that Helen of Sparta was kidnapped by Paris

of Troy. The men of Greece were summoned to take

siege of Troy to protect the woman that launched a

thousand ships. Achilles joins the army when he

was promised great fortune and glory. Patroclus

follows Achilles into the war in hesitation. He is

torn between love and fear for Achilles. The years

that follow tested not only their skills but also their

friendship. Before he is ready, Fate will summon

him to surrender his dear friend into her hand.

Miller's *The Song of Achilles* was awarded the 2012 Orange Prize for Fiction. Her vivid re-magining of *The Illiad* renders a devastating love story with the war of gods and kings as the backdrop. Peace and glory, fame and heart are the themes that resound in Miller's breathtaking rendering of *The Illiad*. *The Song of Achilles* debuts in the *New York Times* bestselling books. It has been translated into Dutch, Mandarin, Japanese, Greek among the other twenty-two languages. Miller was also listed for the 2012 Stonewall Writer of the Year. Her essays and articles appear in the *Guardian*, *Wall Street Journal*, *Lapham's Quarterly* and NPR.org.

In 2018, Miller released her second novel, *Circe*. It debuts as the #1 *New York Times* bestseller. In

Circe, Miller retells the story of the mythologica witch Circe. She was born in the house of gods bu her heart turned to humans for love and acceptance Her fate was dictated by her meddling with witchcraft and a spell she wielded on the human she loved. *Sunday Times* said that as *The Song of Achille.* was a big hit, "*Circe* will be, too."

Bonus Downloads

*Get Free Books with **Any Purchase** of Conversation Starters!*

Every purchase comes with a FREE download!

Add spice to any conversation
Never run out of things to say
Spend time with those you love

Get it Now

or Click Here.

Scan Your Phone

Fireside Questions

"What would you do?"

Tip: These questions can be a fun exercise as it spurs creativity among the readers by allowing alternate scene endings and "if this was you" questions.

~~~

question 21

Miller spent fifteen years as a high school teacher prior to launching her writing career in 2012. How did her experience in teaching hone her writing skills? How did Miller move from the academe to writing?

~~~

question 22

Miller majored in Classics and graduated with a Bachelor's and a Master's degrees from Brown University. *The Song of Achilles* was based on *The Illiad*. *Circe* is based on which of the classics?

question 23

Critics called *Circe* a feminist slant on the classics.
Is Circe a feminist novel? What are the
characteristics of novels to be considered feminist?

~~~

question 24

The NY Times observed that Miller deliberately omitted the story of Circe turning a king into a woodpecker. This was from Ovid's Metamorphoses. Why didn't Miller include this depiction of Circe? If it were included, would it have changed the storyline? How so?

~~~

question 25

ndependent calls Circe a tale with a female lead who :mbodies "empowerment and courage full of :ontemporary resonances". What parts of the novel loes Circe exhibit empowerment and courage? Vhat contemporary resonances does Circe exhibit?

~~~

~~~

question 26

Born into a family of gods, appearance was of keen importance. If you were Circe and you were born with less majestic features, how will you respond to the unfair treatment of your kin? Will you fight back?

~~~

question 27

Circe witnessed the harsh treatment of Prometheus. How would you react when you witness someone being treated the way Prometheus was?

~~~

question 28

Circe delved into witchcraft despite it being prohibited to gods and goddesses alike. If you were Circe and you discovered a power that is forbidden to your kind, will you delve into it or will you avoid it? Why will you do so?

~~~

~~~

question 29

Glaucos is Circe's first and true love but her heart was broken because of Glaucos' infidelity. If you were Circe, will you respond the same way and curse the woman who caused your Glaucos to leave you?

~~~

~~~

question 30

Circe's love for Glaucos caused her to do foolish things. She wielded a spell to make him godlike. Will you wield the same spell on the one you love to ensure your love to last? Why or why not?

~~~

Quiz Questions

"Ready to Announce the Winners?"

Tip: Create a leaderboard and track scores to see who gets the most correct answers. Winners required. Prizes optional.

quiz question 1

Who are the parents of Circe?

~~~

quiz question 2

What is the name of Circe's first human love?

~~~

quiz question 3

Where did Zeus banish Circe?

~~~

quiz question 4

What was the name of the messenger god who passed by Circe's island?

~~~

quiz question 5

True or False: *Circe* is a based on *The Illiad.*

~~~

quiz question 6

True or False: Circe is a witch who lives in the island of Aiaia.

~~~

~~~

quiz question 7

True or False: Scylla is Circe's rival in love.

~~~

quiz question 8

Circe was based on the epic _____.

.~ ~ ~

quiz question 9

Miller's *The Song of Achilles* was based on
_____.

~~~

quiz question 10

True or False: *Circe* is Madeline Miller's first novel.

~~~

quiz question 11

True or False: Most critics reviewed *Circe* as a feminist novel.

~~~

quiz question 12

True or False: Madeline Miller graduated with a Bachelor's Degree in Greek from Brown University.

~~~

Quiz Answers

1. Helios and Perse
2. Glaucos
3. In the island of Aiaia
4. Hermes
5. False
6. True
7. True
8. The Odyssey
9. The Illiad
10. False
11. True
12. False

Ways to Continue Your Reading

EVERY month, our team runs through a wide selection of books to pick the best titles for readers and reading groups, and promotes these titles to our thousands of readers – sometimes with free downloads, sale dates, and additional brochures.

Click here to sign up for these benefits.

If you have not yet read the original work or would like to read it again, you can <u>purchase the original book here.</u>

Bonus Downloads
*Get Free Books with **Any Purchase** of Conversation Starters!*

Every purchase comes with a FREE download!

Add spice to any conversation
Never run out of things to say
Spend time with those you love

or Click Here.

Scan Your Phone

On the Next Page...

If you found this book helpful to your discussions and rate it a 4 or 5, please write us a review on the next page.

Any length would be fine but we'd appreciate hearing you more! We'd be very encouraged.

Till next time,

BookHabits

'Loving Books is Actually a Habit"

36464518R00040

Made in the USA
Middletown, DE
14 February 2019